# Electric Pressure Cooker Cookbook

## Delcious, Quick And Easy To Prepare Electric Pressure Cooker Recipes You Can Cook Tonight!

# Table of Contents

Introduction ........................................................................... 5

## Chapter 1: Electric Pressure Cooker Meal Recipes .... 9

Spring Risotto ........................................................................ 9

Sausages & Mashed Potatoes................................................ 12

Spanish Paella with Seafood, Chicken & Chorizo ............... 14

3 Bean and Italian Sausages .................................................. 17

Whole Chicken with Vegetables ........................................... 20

Spicy Honey Chilli Garlic Chicken....................................... 22

Red Lentil Chili Delight ........................................................ 24

Vegetable Rice Pilaf .............................................................. 26

Beef Stroganoff ..................................................................... 28

Fresh Corn Chowder ............................................................. 31

Chicken Soup ........................................................................ 33

Hawaiian Barbeque Chicken ................................................ 35

Pot Roast ............................................................................... 37

Spicy Chicken........................................................................ 39

Smooth Creamy Mushroom Pork Chops............................. 41

Exotic Cheesy Spaghetti and Meatballs dipped in Sauce.... 43

Delicious Sausages and Healthy Lentils Soup ..................... 46

Unique Three-Bean Salad (Appetizer) ................................. 48

Refreshing Wheat Berry & Vegetable Salad (Appetizer)..... 52

Pasta e Fagioli ................................................................... 55

Pork Barbecue ................................................................ 58

## Chapter 2: Electric Pressure Dessert Recipes ........ 60

Pepper Jelly Lemon Cheesecake ...................................... 60

Coconut Rice Pudding ..................................................... 62

Citrus Yams ..................................................................... 64

Black Rice Pudding ......................................................... 65

Cake ................................................................................. 67

Carrot Pudding ................................................................ 69

Buttery and Cheesy Cap'n Crunch Cheesecake ................ 71

Creamy Pina Colada Rice Pudding .................................. 73

Peanut Butter Cup Cheesecake ........................................ 75

Cooker samoa cheesecake ............................................... 79

Mango Coconut Bread Pudding ....................................... 83

Ginger Steamed Pears and Vanilla Bean Mascarpone Cream ............................................................................... 86

Vanilla Bean Mascarpone Cream ..................................... 89

## Conclusion ............................................................. 90

# Do you want more books?

How would you like books arriving in your inbox each week?

Don't worry they are FREE!

We publish books on all sorts of non-fiction niches and send them out to our subscribers each week to spread the love.

All you have to do is sign up and you're good to go!

Just go to the link at the end of this book, sign up, sit back and wait for your book downloads to arrive!

We couldn't have made it any easier! Enjoy!

# Introduction

Cooking once (for our mothers and grandmothers) was a passion. They would cook your favourite meals involving laborious processes and put lots of love into their food too.

But today's generation is not the same. We don't like to spend as much time in the kitchen, yet are health conscious. Now it is more of a compulsion than a passion and everyone generally lives a hectic schedule and has no time for cooking.

Taste preferences have also changed with time. People are more concerned about health and nutrition; they want convenience as well as speed. The answer to this lies in pressure cooking. It is the cooking method of the day, it is convenient and easy to use and the food is cooked within a short time.

More and more people are slowly discovering the use of pressure cooking and its benefits. Pressure cooking does not create any chemicals which are generally created with baking and grilling.

Studies show that the longer you cook your food, the more liquid you will use and in the process lose more nutrients. High heat damages some of the nutrients of the food but pressure cooking the food heats the food for a shorter time, thereby keeping the nutrition intact.

How does the Pressure Cooker work? When the liquid in the pressure cooker boils, it produces steam and the cooker traps the steam which builds up pressure inside the cooker. This makes the food cook faster and evenly.

The electric pressure cooker is safe and easy to use, it is economical too. It has push button controls, digital displays etc. You can boil, braise, poach, brown, steam, steam roast, stew etc. your food.

I have compiled some easy, nutritious, and healthy recipes for you in this book, I hope you enjoy it!

# © Copyright 2015 by Sammy Nindale
## - All rights reserved.

This document is geared towards providing exact and reliable information in regards to the topic and issue covered. The publication is sold with the idea that the publisher is not required to render accounting, officially permitted, or otherwise, qualified services. If advice is necessary, legal or professional, a practiced individual in the profession should be ordered.

- From a Declaration of Principles which was accepted and approved equally by a Committee of the American Bar Association and a Committee of Publishers and Associations.

In no way is it legal to reproduce, duplicate, or transmit any part of this document in either electronic means or in printed format. Recording of this publication is strictly prohibited and any storage of this document is not allowed unless with written permission from the publisher. All rights reserved.

The information provided herein is stated to be truthful and consistent, in that any liability, in terms of inattention or otherwise, by any usage or abuse of any policies, processes, or directions contained within is the solitary and utter responsibility of the recipient reader. Under no circumstances will any legal responsibility or blame be held against the publisher for any reparation, damages, or monetary loss due to the information herein, either directly or indirectly.

Respective authors own all copyrights not held by the publisher.

The information herein is offered for informational purposes solely, and is universal as so. The presentation of the information is without contract or any type of guarantee assurance.

The trademarks that are used are without any consent, and the publication of the trademark is without permission or backing by the trademark owner. All trademarks and brands within this book are for clarifying purposes only and are the owned by the owners themselves, not affiliated with this document.

Cover image courtesy of Loozrboy – Flickr - https://www.flickr.com/photos/loozrboy/5538139481/

# Chapter 1:
# Electric Pressure Cooker Meal Recipes

## Spring Risotto

**Ingredients:**

- 3 medium shallots chopped
- 1 ½ cups Arborio rice
- 2 - 3 cups low sodium chicken stock
- 1 tablespoon olive oil
- ½ cup white wine
- 1 tablespoon white wine for shallots
- ½ cup frozen peas
- 1 cup asparagus, chopped
- 1 cup baby spinach leaves
- Salt to taste
- Pepper to taste

**For garnish:**

- Chives, chopped
- Parmesan cheese, shredded

**Method:**

1. Press the START button of the pressure cooker so that the heating element is started for browning function.

2. Add a tablespoon of olive oil into the cooker. Add the shallots into the cooker and sauté for a couple of minutes.

3. Add salt, pepper and a tablespoon of white wine. Cook for a couple of minutes more and then press the CANCEL button.

4. Add rice to the cooker along with ½ cup white wine and stock. Stir well. Close the lid and turn it to the LOCK position. Set the pressure valve to airtight. Now press the rice button of the cooker or program it to cook for 10 minutes. When the time is over, it will beep and switch on to the keep warm mode automatically.

5. When cooked, release the pressure. Turn the pressure valve to exhaust.

6. Unlock and open the lid. Allow the keep warm function to stay for a few minutes.

7. Check the consistency of the risotto. The rice should be tender and not sticky or dry. You can add more stock or wine if the desired consistency is not what you want.

8. Add salt, pepper, peas, asparagus, and spinach. Gently fold this into the rice.

9. Close the lid and use the warm function so that the vegetables are cooked (3-5 minutes)

10. Open the lid and add parmesan cheese and chives.
11. Serve hot.

# Sausages & Mashed Potatoes

## Ingredients:

- 4 pork sausages'
- 3 baking potatoes, peeled, diced
- ½ cup milk
- ¼ cup butter, chopped into small pieces or slices
- Salt to taste
- Pepper to taste
- 1 onion, sliced into rings
- ¼ cup sour cream
- ¼ cup parmesan
- A sheet of foil

## Method:

1. Prick the sausages' with a fork all over.
2. Place the potatoes in the bottom of the cooker pot. Add salt and pepper, toss. Add milk and butter.
3. Place a sheet of foil over the potatoes. Place the sausages' over the foil. Top with onions.
4. Close the lid of the pressure cooker and turn it to LOCK position. Set the pressure valve to airtight position. Program it for 20 minutes. When the cooking time is

up, the cooker will beep and go on to the keep warm mode automatically.

5. Release the pressure and open the lid of the cooker.

6. Now remove the sausages' from the foil. The sausages' will look different since it has been cooked.

7. Mash the potatoes with a potato masher directly in the cooker pot. Adjust the consistency and taste of the potatoes by adding more milk, salt and pepper.

8. Serve the potatoes hot with sausage.

# Spanish Paella with Seafood, Chicken & Chorizo

## Ingredients:

- ½ pound chicken
- 4 ounce spicy chorizo
- 1 tablespoon olive oil
- 1 medium onion, diced
- ¼ teaspoon marjoram
- ¼ teaspoon cumin
- A pinch of saffron threads
- 7 ½ ounce long grain rice, uncooked
- 1 cup chicken stock
- ¼ cup water
- ¼ cup white wine
- 2 cloves garlic, minced
- ¼ pound whole shrimps
- ¼ pound clams, with shells, drained
- ¼ cup green peas
- ½ cup bell pepper, diced

- Salt to taste

- Lemon wedges for garnishing

**Method**

1. Press the START button of the pressure cooker so that the heating element is started for browning function.

2. Add a tablespoon of olive oil into the cooker. Add the onions, marjoram, cumin and saffron into the cooker and sauté for a minute.

3. Add chicken and chorizo and sauté until the chorizo starts to separate and everything turns orange in color.

4. Add rice and mix well. Add the chicken stock, wine, salt, and water.

5. Stir well. Close the lid and turn it to the LOCK position. Set the pressure valve to airtight. Now press the rice button of the cooker or program it to cook for 20 minutes. When the time is over, it will beep and switch on to the 'keep warm' mode automatically.

6. When cooked, release the pressure. Turn the pressure valve to exhaust.

7. The lid will now turn and unlock itself. Allow the Keep-warm function to stay for a few minutes.

8. Add garlic and mix gently only at the top part of the rice. Do not mix the rice at the bottom as it needs to be browned.

9. Add shrimps, peas, bell peppers, and clam. Mix it into the rice.

10. Close the lid again and lock it. Press START.

11. When the liquid contents in the cooker have dried up, the temperature will rise and the cooker will automatically shut off. It will go to the Keep-warm mode.

12. After about 10 minutes open the lid and check if the clams and shrimps are cooked. If not, repeat step 10 and 11 again.

13. Serve hot with lemon juice and lemon wedges.

# 3 Bean and Italian Sausages

## Ingredients:

- 1 package spicy Italian sausage, separated and crumbled
- 1 tablespoon olive oil
- 1 onion, finely chopped
- 2 stalks celery, finely chopped
- ½ cup corn, fresh or frozen
- 2 Serrano chilies, finely chopped
- 2 cloves garlic, finely chopped
- ½ tablespoon dried basil
- ½ tablespoon dried oregano
- ½ cup pinto beans, dried
- ½ cup kidney beans, dried
- ½ cup black beans dried
- ½ a can of beer
- 2 cups chicken stock
- ½ can whole tomatoes
- ½ can tomato sauce
- Salt to taste

- Pepper to taste

**For Garnishing:**

- 2 tablespoons sour cream or plain yogurt
- ¼ cup parmesan cheese, shredded
- 2 tablespoons fresh basil

**Method:**

1. Press the START button of the pressure cooker so that the heating element is started for browning function.
2. Add a tablespoon of olive oil into the cooker. Add the onions, celery, chilli, corn, and garlic into the cooker and sauté for a couple of minutes.
3. Add sausages', basil, oregano, salt, and pepper. Sauté for 4-5 minutes and then press the CANCEL button.
4. Add the 3 beans and stir well. Add water, stock, and beer. The liquid should be at least an inch above the ingredients of the cooker. If not adjust by adding water to it.
5. Stir well. Close the lid and turn it to the LOCK position. Set the pressure valve to airtight. Program it to cook for 75 minutes. When the time is over, it will beep and switch on to the Keep-warm mode automatically.
6. When cooked, release the pressure. Turn the pressure valve to exhaust.
7. The lid will now turn and unlock itself. Allow the Keep-warm function to stay for a few minutes.

8. Add chilli and stir well. Check the consistency of the ingredients in the cooker. If it seems too dry, add some chicken stock. Taste and adjust salt and pepper to taste.

9. To serve, garnish with sour cream, parmesan, and basil.

10. Serve hot and immediately.

# Whole Chicken with Vegetables

## Ingredients:

- 1 whole chicken
- 1 ½ cups chicken broth
- ½ cup carrots, chopped
- ½ cup beans, chopped
- ½ cup broccoli floret's
- ½ cup peas
- ½ cup potatoes, chopped
- Salt to taste
- Pepper to taste
- Chilli flakes to taste (optional)

## Method:

1. Place the chicken in the pot of the pressure cooker. Add broth, salt and pepper. Mix well and add the vegetables.

2. Close the lid of the pressure cooker and turn it to LOCK position. Set the pressure valve to airtight position. Program it for 30 minutes. When the cooking time is up, the cooker will beep and go on to the keep warm mode automatically.

3. Release the pressure and open the lid of the cooker.

4. Mix well and serve hot with rice or pasta or mashed potatoes.

# Spicy Honey Chilli Garlic Chicken

## Ingredients:

- 1 ½ pounds chicken thighs, skinless, boneless
- 1 teaspoon garlic, minced
- 1 teaspoon Sriracha chili garlic sauce
- 6 tablespoons soy sauce
- 6 tablespoons tomato ketchup
- 6 tablespoons honey
- 1 tablespoon corn starch
- 1 tablespoon water
- 1 tablespoon fresh basil, chopped

## Method:

1. Place the chicken in the pot of the pressure cooker. Add garlic, chili sauce, soy sauce, tomato ketchup, and honey. Mix well.

2. Close the lid of the pressure cooker and turn it to LOCK position. Set the pressure valve to airtight position. Program it for 9 minutes. After 9 minutes, release the pressure and open the lid.

3. Meanwhile mix together in a bowl corn starch and water. Add it to the cooker pot. Stir constantly until mixed well.

4. Select SIMMER mode and bring to a boil. Stir constantly until the sauce thickens.

5. Add basil and mix well.

6. Mix well and serve hot with rice.

# Red Lentil Chili Delight

**Ingredients:**

- ½ pound red lentils
- 3 ½ cups water, divided
- 1 can (14.5 ounce) salt free tomatoes(preferably fire roasted), diced
- ½ a 6 ounce can salt free tomato paste
- 1 medium onion, chopped
- 1 large red bell pepper, chopped
- 1 ½ ounce pitted dates
- 4 cloves garlic, minced
- 2 tablespoons apple cider vinegar
- ¾ tablespoon parsley flakes
- ¾ tablespoon oregano
- ¾ tablespoon chilli powder or to taste
- 1 teaspoon smoked paprika
- ¼ teaspoon chipotle chilli powder
- Red chilli flakes to taste

**Method:**

1. Blend together dates, garlic, bell pepper, tomatoes, and ½ cup water in a mixer until smooth.

2. Place the rest of the ingredients in the pressure cooker. Add the blended dates paste.

3. Close the lid of the pressure cooker and turn it to LOCK position. Set the pressure valve to airtight position. Program it for 10 minutes. Let the pressure release naturally and open the lid.

4. Serve hot immediately

# Vegetable Rice Pilaf

## Ingredients:

- ½ tablespoon butter
- 1 small onion, chopped
- 1 stalk celery, chopped
- 1 medium carrot, chopped
- 1 cup long grain white rice, washed and drained
- 7 ounce vegetable broth or chicken broth
- 10 tablespoons water
- Salt to taste
- ½ cup frozen peas, thawed
- 1 tablespoon parsley, finely chopped
- ¼ cup almonds, sliced, toasted

## Method:

1. Press the START button of the pressure cooker so that the heating element is started for browning function.
2. Add butter into the cooker. Add the onions, celery, and carrot and sauté for a couple of minutes.
3. Add rice and sauté until rice becomes opaque. Add water, salt, and broth. Close the lid and turn to the LOCK position.

4. Select High pressure mode and program for 3 minutes. When it switches off wait for 5 minutes and release pressure and open the lid.

5. Fluff the rice with a fork. Add peas, parsley, and almonds. Mix gently and serve hot immediately.

# Beef Stroganoff

## Ingredients:

- 1 pound beef round steak, cut into 1 inch pieces
- ½ tablespoon vegetable oil
- 1 medium onion, chopped
- 2 cloves garlic, minced
- 1 tablespoon tomato paste
- ¾ cup beef broth
- ½ tablespoon butter + ½ tablespoon vegetable oil
- 6 ounces white mushrooms, sliced
- 1 tablespoon cornstarch
- 1 ½ tablespoon cold water
- 3 tablespoons sour cream
- Salt to taste
- Pepper to taste
- Egg noodles, cooked

## Method:

1. Sprinkle beef with salt and pepper generously.

2. Press the START button of the pressure cooker so that the heating element is started for browning function.

3. Add oil into the cooker. When oil is heated, add beef and brown it. Add more oil if needed. When brown, remove and keep aside on a plate.

4. Add the onions, sauté for a couple of minutes until the onions are brown

5. Add garlic and tomato paste. Sauté for a few seconds.

6. Add beef broth, browned beef and any juices of the browned beef. Close the lid and turn to the LOCK position.

7. Select High Pressure and program for 15 minutes.

8. Meanwhile, place a sauté pan over medium heat. Add butter and oil.

9. When butter melts, add mushrooms and sauté until brown. Add salt and pepper.

10. When the pressure cooker switches off, let the pressure release naturally for 10 minutes. After that release the left over steam.

11. In a small bowl mix together cornstarch and water until smooth. Add this to the cooker pot stirring constantly.

12. Select the SIMMER mode and bring to a boil. Stir continuously until the sauce becomes thick.

13. Add 3 tablespoons of the gravy to sour cream and mix well. Add this to the gravy and mix well all the ingredients of the cooker.

14. Add the sautéed mushrooms. Mix well.

15. Serve hot over egg noodles.

# Fresh Corn Chowder

## Ingredients:

- 3 fresh corn cobs
- 2 tablespoons butter
- ¼ cup onions, chopped
- 1 ½ cups water
- 1 medium sized potato, diced
- 1 tablespoon dried parsley
- 1 tablespoon cornstarch
- 1 tablespoon water
- 1 ½ cups half and half OR milk
- A pinch of cayenne pepper, ground
- 2 slices cooked bacon, diced
- Salt to taste
- Pepper to taste

## Method:

1. With a knife, remove the corn kernels.
2. Press the START button of the pressure cooker so that the heating element is started for browning function.

3. Add butter into the cooker. Add othe onions and sauté for a couple of minutes.

4. Add water and the corn cobs. Close the lid of the pressure cooker and turn to LOCK position. Select High Pressure and program for 10 minutes. When the cooker gets switched off, release the pressure in the cooker.

5. Discard the corn cobs and retain the broth in the cooker itself.

6. Place a steamer basket in the pressure cooker. Place potatoes and corn on the basket. Close the lid of the pressure cooker. Select High Pressure and program for 4 minutes.

7. When the pressure cooker switches off, release the pressure. Remove the steaming basket from the cooker.

8. In a small bowl, mix together cornstarch and a tablespoon of water.

9. Select the SIMMER mode. Add the cornstarch mixture to the cooker, stirring constantly until the soup is thick. (If you are using milk, then add one more tablespoon of cornstarch and water).

10. Add bacon, half, and half, corn, potatoes, salt and pepper. Heat thoroughly but do not boil.

# Chicken Soup

## Ingredients:

- 3 cups water
- 2 teaspoons instant chicken bouillon
- ½ teaspoons celery seeds
- ½ teaspoon onion salt
- 1 small bunch parsley
- Pepper powder to taste
- 2 chicken breasts or leg quarters or turkey meat
- 1 cup onions, chopped
- 1 cup carrots, diced
- 1 cup celery, diced
- 1 cup squash, cooked, pureed (you can use pumpkin puree)
- 4 ounce egg noodles, cook according to instructions on the package
- 1 can cream of mushroom soup
- Salt to taste
- Pepper to taste

**Method:**

1. Press the START button of the pressure cooker so that the heating element is started for browning function.

2. Add all the ingredients except the cream of mushroom soup and noodles.

3. Close the lid of the pressure cooker and turn to the LOCK position. Select High Pressure and program for 20 minutes. When the cooker switches off, release the pressure in the cooker.

4. Remove the chicken pieces out. Remove the bones from the chicken and chop the chicken into smaller pieces.

5. Put the chicken pieces back to the cooker pot. Add cream of mushroom soup.

6. Select SIMMER mode. Stir occasionally. Add boiled noodles to it. Heat thoroughly.

7. Serve hot with fresh bread.

# Hawaiian Barbeque Chicken

**Ingredients:**

- 1 ½ pound chicken, fresh or frozen, de skinned
- ½ cup BBQ sauce
- 1 cup pineapples, fresh or canned, diced
- ½ cup coconut milk
- ½ tablespoon red chilli flakes or to taste
- Juice of a lime for garnish

**Method:**

1. Mix together in a bowl, BBQ sauce, milk, and chilli flakes.
2. Place the pineapple at the bottom of the cooker pot.
3. Dip the chicken pieces in the BBQ sauce mixture and place above the pineapple layer. Pour the sauce over the chicken pieces if remaining.
4. Close the lid of the cooker. Turn it to LOCK position. Set the pressure valve to airtight and program for 10 minutes.
5. When the cooker switches off, release the pressure. Unlock and open the lid of the cooker.
6. Remove the chicken pieces from the pot and keep aside.

7. Press the START button of the pressure cooker so that the heating element is started for browning function.

8. Simmer until the liquid in the pot thickens to a saucy consistency you desire.

9. Now add the chicken pieces back to the pot. Mix well. Press the CANCEL button.

10. Serve hot garnished with lime juice.

# Pot Roast

## Ingredients:

- 2 ½ pound rump roast
- Salt to taste
- Pepper to taste
- 2 tablespoon all purpose flour
- ½ tablespoon extra virgin olive oil
- 1 yellow onion, cut into ¼ inch slices
- ¾ cup beef stock
- 2 cloves garlic, crushed
- 2 sprigs fresh thyme
- 1 bay leaf
- Salt to taste
- Pepper to taste

## Method:

1. Place the flour in a large bowl. Add the roast. Sprinkle salt and pepper. Toss well to coat evenly.
2. Press the START button of the pressure cooker so that the heating element is started for browning function.

3. Add olive oil. When the oil is nearly smoking, add the roast and brown it on all the sides. Remove the roast and keep on a plate.

4. Add onions to the pot of the cooker and sauté until tender.

5. Add the roast back to the pot. Also add carrots, stock, garlic, bay leaf, and thyme.

6. Close the lid. Turn to LOCK position.

7. Select High Pressure and program for 80 minutes. When the cooker gets switched off, release the pressure in the cooker.

8. Remove the roast on to a cutting board and cool for around 5 minutes. Slice the meat and place on the serving platter.

9. Discard the thyme and bay leaf from the sauce in the pot. Pour the vegetables along with the liquid over the roast. Season with salt and pepper.

# Spicy Chicken

**Ingredients:**

- 3 medium onions
- 4 cloves garlic
- ½ inch piece of ginger
- ½ chicken cut into 6 pieces
- 3 cardamoms
- 3 cloves
- 1 star anise
- 1 stick cinnamon around 2 inches
- ¼ cup tomato puree
- 1 tablespoon chilli paste
- 1 tomato, quartered
- 1 carrot, sliced into 2 inch sticks
- ½ cup yogurt
- ½ cup water
- Salt to taste
- ½ teaspoon sugar
- ½ cup peas

- ½ tablespoon cilantro, chopped

- 1 tablespoon fried onions

**Method:**

1. Place all the ingredients except yogurt, peas, and cilantro in the pot of the pressure cooker.

11. Close the lid of the cooker. Turn it to LOCK position. Set the pressure valve to airtight and program for 20 minutes.

2. When the cooker switches off, release the pressure. Unlock and open the lid of the cooker.

3. Add peas, yogurt, and cilantro. Mix well and serve immediately with rice

# Smooth Creamy Mushroom Pork Chops

**Ingredients:**

- 6 pork chops
- 1½ cups water
- 1 can cream of mushroom soup
- 1 ½ cups sour cream
- Salt and Pepper to Taste
- 2-3 tablespoon oil (vegetable oil preferred)
- 1 cup chopped mushroom (optional)

**For Garnish:**

- 1 tablespoon chopped parsley

**Method:**

1. Turn 'ON' the Electric Pressure Cooker.
2. Add oil and heat it on medium flame.
3. After heating the oil, sprinkle some pepper and salt on both sides of the pork chips. Keep it at the bottom of your electric cooker.
4. Keep on turning the porn chips until they get lightly browned on both the sides. Keep checking it from time to time to see if the pork chips are sautéed properly.

5. Once the pork chips are lightly browned, keep aside on the platter.

6. Add water in the cooker to deglaze any remaining chunks and bits of the pork.

7. Now add cream of mushroom soup, sour cream and mushrooms in the cooker. Heat it over medium flame.

8. Close the lid of the cooker and set the timer for 3-4 minutes on High Pressure.

9. Once the timer is 'off', open the lid and add pork chops.

10. Let it simmer for about 8 minutes on medium flame to absorb the contents of the sauce.

11. Turn 'OFF' the cooker; remove the pork chops and gravy in the platter.

12. Sprinkle salt and pepper.

13. Garnish over the top with chopped parsley.

# Exotic Cheesy Spaghetti and Meatballs dipped in Sauce

## Ingredients:

### For Meatballs:

- ½ pound ground pork
- 1 cup fresh bread crumbs
- 1 pound ground beef
- ½ cup grated parmesan cheese
- 1 large egg, beaten
- 2 cloves garlic, minced
- Pepper and salt to taste
- Olive oil

### For the Sauce:

- 1 tablespoon Olive oil
- 1 cup chopped onion
- 1 can crushed tomatoes (or tomato puree/ chopped tomatoes)
- ½ teaspoon red chili flakes
- 3-4 cloves garlic, minced or chopped

- 1 tablespoon chopped parsley
- 10-15 basil leaves, chopped
- Salt and Pepper to taste
- 1 ½ pounds spaghetti

**For Garnishing:**

- Freshly grated Parmesan

**Method:**

1. Take a bowl and add ground beef, ground pork, beaten egg, bread crumbs, parmesan cheese, garlic, salt and pepper in it.
2. Form a mixture and combine the ingredients with your hands so that all the ingredients are properly blended and mixed.
3. Use your hands to make the balls from the mixture.
4. Set the mode for 'browning' after turning on your electric pressure cooker.
5. Add olive oil in the cooker and let it heat up.
6. Once the oil is hot, carefully place the balls in the cooker. Brown the meatballs from all the sides by regularly moving them around with a fork.
7. Remove the balls once browned.
8. Clean the cooker to remove the chunks of meatballs.

9. Add olive oil in it and let it settle till hot.

10. Add onions and sauté it till it turns translucent and golden brown in colour.

11. Add minced or chopped garlic and cook for 1 minute.

12. Now add tomato puree, herbs, chilli flakes, salt and pepper.

13. Add some water in the mixture for giving more consistency to the sauce. Then add the spaghetti in it.

14. Add the meatballs in the sauce.

15. Cover the lid of the cooker and set the timer for around 12-15 minutes on High Pressure.

16. Once the timer is 'OFF', you'll hear a 'beep sound' which indicates the Timer. Let the pressure settle down by itself and then open the lid of the cooker.

17. Take a platter and transfer the content on it.

18. Garnish the spaghetti and meatballs with grated parmesan cheese on the top.

# Delicious Sausages and Healthy Lentils Soup

**Ingredients:**

- 1 ½ cup sausages, chopped
- 2-3 tablespoon oil
- ¾ cup dried lentils (mixed preferable)
- 6 cups fresh water
- 4 garlic cloves, minced
- 2 cups tomatoes, crushed
- 1 cup mixture of onions, carrot and celery.
- 2-3 Bay leaves
- Salt and Pepper to taste

**Method:**

1. Turn 'ON' the electric pressure cooker and set on the Browning mode.
2. Pour some oil in the cooker. Add onion, bay leaves and garlic and sauté it till onions turns golden brown in color.
3. Then add carrot and celery in the cooker. Sauté the mixture until the ingredients gives a strong aroma.
4. Turn 'OFF' the browning mode, and then add crushed tomatoes in the cooker.

5. Keep mixing the ingredients till the tomatoes are completely broken down into gravy.

6. Add water later on, and when the water starts to boil, add dried lentils and sausages.

7. Cover the lid of your electric cooker and set the timer for 12-15 minutes.

8. To get perfectly blended lentils, let the pressure settle down gradually once the timer is off.

9. Open the lid after all the pressure is released naturally and stir the soup.

10. Remove the soup in the bowl and serve hot.

# Unique Three-Bean Salad (Appetizer)

## Ingredients:

- 3 tbsp. sherry vinegar
- 1 tbsp. fresh lime juice
- 1 ½ tbsp. low sodium soy sauce
- 1 ½ tbsp. honey
- 1 ½ tsp precisely cleaved fresh ginger
- 1 tsp Asian chili paste and garlic
- 2/3 cup vegetable oil
- 4 ears fresh corn, silks and husks removed
- 8 ounces of green beans, chopped into pieces of ½ inches on the diagonal
- 1 cup pink, black, pinto or cannellini beans, washed, drained and gathered over
- 1 cup cut red bell pepper (1/2 x ¼ inch strips)
- 1 cup thinly cup celery
- ¾ cup preserved/dry cranberries
- ½ cup cut red onion
- Freshly ground pepper and kosher salt for taste

**Method:**

1. Place lime juice, sherry vinegar, honey, soy sauce, chili paste and ginger in a medium sized bowl.
2. Whisk to combine and add oil in a steady and slow stream.
3. Keep whisking until a cream is formed.
4. You can do the above steps in a food processor or a blender as well.
5. You will obtain 1 cup vinaigrette dressing.
6. Let it stand while you prepare the remaining salad.
7. Allow the flavors to mix.
8. Place rack/trivet in the cooking pot and place cork on it.
9. Add a cup of water in the cooking pot.
10. Choose 'High' pressure on the cooking pot and set the time for 1 minute.
11. On hearing the beep sound, use Quick Pressure Release.
12. Remove the corn and quick drop into a bowl of ice water for stopping the cooking.
13. Put the green beans on a 16" square sheet of paper (parchment paper) and get its corners together.
14. Place a rack/rivet.
15. Select the 'High Pressure' and set the time for 1 min.

16. When the beep sound comes, use the Quick Pressure Release of your Electric cooker.

17. Remove the green beans and quick drop into a bowl of ice water for stopping the cooking.

18. Place a rack/rivet.

19. Put edamame in the cooking pot.

20. Mix it in hot water for about half a minute.

21. Remove and quickly drop into ice water bowl to stop cooking.

22. Wash all the vegetables.

23. Drain them by putting on layered paper towels for full drain.

24. Add 2 cups of water in the water in the cooking pot. Then add dried beans to the pot.

25. Select 'High Pressure' on your electric cooker and set the cooking time for 11 min.

26. When you hear the beep sound, use Natural Pressure Release.

27. In case you find it to be not fully tender, select 'simmer' and simmer it till it become tender.

28. Drain it. Plunge it into ice water and then drain again.

29. Cut the corns from cobs and keep in a large bowl with dried cranberries, red pepper and red onions.

30. Now add cooked pink beans (drained) and 2/3 vinaigrette.

31. In case it has separated, stir with whisk.

32. Move it back and forth in gentle motion to combine.

33. Cover it and put it for refrigeration in case you are not planning to serve it immediately.

34. Stir edamame and green beans into the salad before serving.

35. Decorate it in a bowl for serving.

# Refreshing Wheat Berry & Vegetable Salad (Appetizer)

## Ingredients:

- 1 1/2 cups wheat berries
- 1 ½ tbsp. vegetable oil
- 6 ¾ cups of water
- ¼ cup chopped onion (red)
- 1 ½ tsp Dijon-style mustard
- ½ tsp freshly ground black pepper
- 1 tsp kosher salt
- ¼ cup white balsamic / fruit flavored vinegar
- 1 tsp sugar
- ½ cup extra virgin olive oil
- 1 cup shredded zucchini
- 1 1/3 cups cut corn (use thawed- frozen)
- ¾ cup chopped red bell pepper
- 1/3 cup chopped sun dried tomatoes
- ½ cup chopped green onion
- ¼ cup chopped fresh parsley

**Method:**

1. Place water, wheat berries and vegetable oil in the cooking pot of your electric pressure cooker.

2. Cap and lock the lid properly in place.

3. Select 'High Pressure' on your electric cooker and set the timer for 50 min.

4. On hearing the beep sound, turn it off.

5. Release the pressure with the help of 'Quick Pressure Release'.

6. Turn off when the float vale drops.

7. Now, remove the lid carefully, bending away from you to allow dispersing of the steam.

8. Check the grains, if they are yet chewy, select 'simmer' and keep cooking till it is done to taste.

9. Drain the wheat berries.

10. Transfer the wheat berries to a big bowl.

11. Prepare the dressing while cooking the wheat berries.

12. Now, place mustard, red onion, remaining half tsp salt, sugar, vinegar and pepper in the work bowl of a mini food processor or a food processor fitted with the metal chopping blade and keep the procedure on until it becomes smooth.

13. Pour oil and process till it emulsifies. There should be about 7/8 cup dressing.

14. On cooling of the wheat berries, add half a cup of dressing. (You can take the quantity as per your taste too) and toss for coating.

15. Now add zucchini, corn, chopped green onion, red pepper and sun-dried tomatoes.

16. Toss in a gentle manner for combining.

17. Add parsley.

18. Flip to combine.

19. In case you are not serving it immediately, cover it and put it for refrigeration.

20. Remove from the refrigerator half an hour before serving.

# Pasta e Fagioli

## Ingredients:

- 1 tbsp. extra virgin olive oil
- 1-half cups chopped onion
- Half a cup sliced celery
- 1 cup diced carrot (Half inch)
- 3 cloves of garlic, skinned and chopped up
- 2 tsp Italian herb blend, detached
- 1 pound white beans or dry cannellini, washed and picked over
- Water- 6 cups
- Bay leaf- 1 no.
- 4 cups stock/chicken broth or low sodium vegetable
- 14 ounce (2 cans) diced tomatoes with juices
- 1 tsp sea or kosher salt
- 1- half cup tubetti, small shell pasta or small macaroni
- Chopped fresh parsley
- Freshly shaved, shredded and grated cheese

**Method:**

1. Select Sauté and pour oil in the cooking pot.

2. Heat the oil for 3-4 min.

3. Add chopped onions, celery, carrots, garlic and one tsp of Italian herb blend when the oil gets heated up.

4. Sauté, moving for 4-5 min, until the onions gets translucent and softened.

5. Now add water, bay leaf and dried beans.

6. Cover the lid and lock it in place.

7. Select 'High Pressure' on your electric cooker and set the timer for about 35 min.

8. When you hear the beep sound, allow the pressure to release on its own, about 20 min.

9. On dropping of the float valve, turn it off. Remove the lid, bending away from you for allowing dispersing of the steam.

10. Stir in stock/broth, tomatoes along with their juices and the rest of the tsp of Italian herb blend.

11. Choose Brown.

12. When the liquids start boiling, add pasta to it and cook according to the directions on the package.

13. Turn for keeping warn for holding soup until prepared for serving.

14. Discard on removing the bay leaf before serving.

15. Distribute in warmed bowls with the garnishing of freshly chopped parsley and shaved, shredded and grated cheese.

# Pork Barbecue

## Ingredients:

- Half tbsp vegetable oil
- 4 pounds country style pork shoulder slices or spare ribs
- 1 big onion, sliced and peeled
- Half cup cider vinegar
- 2 tbsp brown sugar
- 1 tsp salt
- Half tsp freshly ground black pepper
- 2 cups barbecue sauce (purchased or homemade)

## Method:

1. Take oil in your cooking pot and choose 'Browning'.
2. When the oil gets heated, add pork in it.
3. Brown it well on all the sides in number of batches.
4. Add vinegar, onion, salt, brown sugar and pepper in the cooking pot along with the browned pork and any kind of juices which may be accumulated.
5. Cover the lid and lock it in place.
6. Choose 'High Pressure' and set the timer for 45 min.

7. Allow natural release of pressure on the beep sound.

8. Turn it off.

9. Remove the lid, bending away from you for allowing the dispersion of steam.

10. Let the pork cool in cooling liquid.

11. When it gets cooled enough to be handled, remove the pork from the bones, get rid of the pork fat and the bones.

12. Filter the cooking liquid and reserve half cup.

13. Keep the pork in the cooking pot along with barbecue sauce and the half cup reserved cooking liquid.

14. Cover the lid and lock it in place.

15. Select 'Low Pressure' and set the timer for 3 min.

16. Use the Quick Pressure Release for releasing the pressure on the sound of beep.

17. Remove the lid, bending away from you for allowing the dispersion of steam.

18. It is ready to be served hot!

19. You can serve it on sliced buns for the sandwiches.

# Chapter 2:
# Electric Pressure Dessert Recipes

## Pepper Jelly Lemon Cheesecake

**Ingredients:**

**For the crust:**

- 3 sheets Graham crackers, crumbled
- 1 cup macaroon cookies, crumbled
- 1 tablespoon butter

**For the filling:**

- 8 ounce cream cheese at room temperature
- ¼ cup sugar
- 1 egg
- 1 tablespoon fresh lemon juice
- ½ tablespoon grated lemon zest
- ½ teaspoon vanilla extract
- 1 tablespoon habanero peppery jelly

**Method:**

1. Mix together the crumbled macaroon cookies, crackers and butter.

2. Take a baking pan, smaller than the size of your cooker. Grease the base of the baking pan with butter.

3. Lay the crumbled mixture in the baking pan. Press well. Keep aside.

4. To make the filling: Place cream cheese and sugar in a bowl. Beat well with a stick blender. Add rest of the ingredients. Beat well until smooth and creamy.

5. Pour this mixture over the crust in the baking pan. Spread evenly.

6. Pour 2-3 cups of water in the bottom of the pressure cookers pot. Place a trivet in the pot.

7. Cover the baking pan with a sheet of foil. Now place the baking pan on the trivet inside the pot.

8. Close the lid of the pressure cooker and turn it to LOCK position. Adjust the valve to airtight. Select High Pressure and program for 15 minutes. When the cooker gets switched off, let the pressure release naturally.

9. Unlock the lid and open it. Let the cheese cake cool in the cooker for a while.

10. Remove after a while and let cool further.

11. Serve warm or if you like chilled, refrigerate.

# Coconut Rice Pudding

## Ingredients:

- ½ cup Arborio rice
- 1 ½ cups coconut milk, unsweetened
- 1 cup almond milk, unsweetened
- ½ cup water
- 2 sticks cinnamon
- ¼ teaspoon freshly ground cloves
- 1 whole vanilla bean
- 2 orange zest strips
- 1 can condensed milk, sweetened

## For garnishing:

- Honey
- Strawberries, sliced
- Blueberries
- A large pinch of ground nutmeg

## Method:

1. Pour coconut milk, almond milk, and water into the pot of the pressure cooker.

2. Press the START button of the pressure cooker so that the heating element is started.

3. Add cloves, cinnamon and orange zest strips. Split the vanilla pod with a knife and scrape all the vanilla beans out and add to the pot. Add the vanilla pod too.

4. Let the mixture simmer for a while. Now press the CANCEL button to switch off the machines heating element.

5. Add rice to the pot and mix well.

6. Close the lid of the pressure cooker and lock it. Adjust the pressure value to airtight. Program the cooker for 15 minutes.

7. When the machine switches off after 15 minutes, let the pressure release naturally.

8. Open the lock and remove the lid. Discard the vanilla pod, cinnamon and orange zest strips.

9. Add the condensed milk and mix well.

10. Serve either warm or refrigerate if you like it cold.

11. To serve, garnish with honey. Sprinkle nutmeg and serve with strawberries and blueberries.

# Citrus Yams

## Ingredients:

- 1 cup orange juice
- 1 ½ tablespoons orange zest
- ¾ cup brown sugar or to taste
- 1 tablespoon butter
- 2 yams, slice in half lengthwise
- ¼ teaspoon salt

## Method:

1. Place the yams facing up in the bottom of the pot of the pressure cooker. Pour orange juice.

2. Sprinkle with salt and half the orange zest. Sprinkle each piece with about a tablespoon of brown sugar (use only half the brown sugar).

3. Close the lid of the pressure cooker and turn to LOCK position. Program it for 7 minutes.

4. When the cooker switches off, then release the pressure in the cooker. Open the lock and remove the lid.

5. Mash the yams with a potato masher. Add butter, remaining brown sugar, and remaining orange zest. Mix together and mash it further.

6. Serve warm.

# Black Rice Pudding

**Ingredients:**

- ½ cup black rice
- ¾ cup water
- ½ tablespoon butter
- ¼ teaspoon salt
- ½ cup milk
- ¼ cup sugar
- 6 tablespoons half and half
- 1 egg, beaten
- ½ teaspoon vanilla extract
- 1/3 cup dried cherries

**Method:**

1. Add rice to the pot of the pressure cooker. Also add water, butter, and salt. Close the lid and turn to LOCK position. Select High pressure and program for 22 minutes.

2. When the cooker switches off, wait for 10 minutes to release pressure naturally and then release the remaining pressure. Unlock and open the lid.

3. Add milk and sugar to the pot. Mix thoroughly with the rest of the ingredients in the pot and the sugar is dissolved.

4. Select SIMMER mode

5. Whisk together egg and half and half in a bowl. Add this to the pot after passing through a fine strainer. Continue cooking stirring constantly until the mixture just begins to boil.

6. Switch off the pressure cooker and add the cherries and mix well.

7. If you like it hot, serve immediately else cool it in the refrigerator and serve chilled.

# Cake

**Ingredients:**

- 100 grams self rising flour
- 100 grams castor sugar
- 10 grams unsweetened cocoa powder
- ½ teaspoon baking powder
- ¼ teaspoon baking soda
- ½ teaspoon salt
- 2 ½ tablespoons butter
- 100 ml warm water
- ½ tablespoon fresh lemon or lime juice
- ½ teaspoon vanilla essence

**Method:**

1. Sift together all the dry ingredients and place in a large bowl along with sugar.
2. Melt butter in a small pan and leave it to cool.
3. In another bowl add warm water, lemon juice, and vanilla essence. Mix well.
4. Pour the water mixture into the bowl of dry ingredients. Mix well, add melted butter and stir until well combined. Do not over-beat.

5. Grease the cooking pot with butter and pour the batter into the pot.

6. Gently place the pot into the cooker.

7. Close the lid and turn to LOCK position. Switch the valve on the lid to BAKE position. Bake for around 30 minutes.

8. When cooled slightly invert the cake on to a plate. Slice when it cools further.

# Carrot Pudding

## Ingredients:

- 4 cups red carrots, grated
- 1 ½ cups milk
- ½ cup sugar
- 3 tablespoons ghee (you can use unsalted butter too)
- 20 cashew nuts, chop each into 3-4 pieces
- 4 tablespoons raisins
- ½ teaspoon grounded cardamom

## Method:

1. Press the START button of the pressure cooker so that the heating element is started.
2. Add 1 tablespoon of ghee to the pot of the pressure cooker. Add raisins, sauté until they puff up. Remove and keep aside. Add cashew, sauté until light brown, remove and keep aside.
3. Add the remaining ghee to the pot. Add carrots and sauté for 3-4 minutes.
4. Add milk.
5. Close the lid and turn to LOCK position. Select High pressure and program for 10 minutes.

6. When the cooker switches off, let the pressure release naturally. Unlock and open the lid.

7. Set on SIMMER mode. Simmer until the liquid dries up.

8. Now add sugar and continue cooking until the sugar is melted and the pudding is thick.

9. Add the cardamom, roasted cashew, and raisins and cook for a few seconds more.

10. Press CANCEL and switch off the cooker.

11. Serve hot or warm but not cold.

# Buttery and Cheesy Cap'n Crunch Cheesecake

**Ingredients:**

**For The Crust:**

- 1 cup Cap'n Crunch cereal
- 5 tablespoon unsalted melted butter

**For the Cheesecake:**

- 1 pound cream cheese
- 2 eggs
- ½ cup sugar
- ¼ cup sour cream
- 1 teaspoon vanilla extract
- 1 ½ tablespoon flour

**Method:**

1. Take the electric pressure cooker.
2. Place the rack in the pressure cooker. Add water in it (Be careful with the water content as to keep it below the level of the rack).
3. Take some foil and fold it in a way to easily place a pan in the cooker and you can also easily remove the pan without much trouble.

4. Use the butter and rub the bottom and sides of the spring form pan.

5. Take a bowl and mix the cereals and melted butter so that all the cereal crumbs are properly coated with butter.

6. Take the buttered cereals and place it in the bottom of the pan.

7. Use the cream cheese and sugar in the food processor and blend it to form a smoothie. While processing, add the eggs one by one for making sure that the smoothie is mixed properly.

8. Then add the sour cream, vanilla extract and flour in the mixture. Process it for one more minute.

9. Once the smoothie is properly processed, pour over the batter in the pan.

10. Use to foil to lower the pan in the cooker.

11. Cover the lid of your electric cooker and turn 'ON' the timer for 24-27 min.

12. Let the pressure reduce naturally for about 5-10 minutes when the timer is 'OFF',

13. Remove the lid and carefully take out the pan.

14. Put the cheesecake in the refrigerator to let it cool for about 5 hours minimum.

15. Remove the cheesecake from the refrigerator and serve it.

# Creamy Pina Colada Rice Pudding

## Ingredients:

- 1 ½ cups water
- 1 cup Arborio rice
- 1 tbsp. coconut oil
- ¼ tsp salt
- Half a cup sugar
- 1 14-oz can coconut milk
- Half cup milk
- 2 eggs
- Half tsp vanilla extract
- 1 can pineapple- cut in half and well drained

## Method:

1. Blend rice, oil, water and salt in the pressure cooker pot.
2. Lock the lid of the cooker in place.
3. Select the 'High' Pressure
4. Select the cooking time for 3 minutes.
5. Turn of the pressure cooker on the sound of 'Beep'

6. Release the halting pressure with the quick pressure release feature in your electric pressure cooker.

7. Add sugar and coconut oil to the rice in the pressure cooker pot.

8. Stir to mix.

9. Whisk the eggs with vanilla and milk in a small mixing bowl.

10. Pour this mix through a fine mesh strainer in the pressure cooking pot.

11. Select 'Sauté' in your cooker and cook while stirring constantly.

12. Stir it till the mixture starts boiling.

13. Turn off the electric pressure cooker.

14. Blend the pineapple tidbits.

15. Stream in the serving dishes and relax.

16. Pudding will start thickening as it cools.

17. The pudding is ready to be served with the toppings of toasted coconut, whipped cream and maraschino cherry.

# Peanut Butter Cup Cheesecake

## Ingredients

- 1 cup crushed crumbs of Oreo cookie
- 2 tbsp melted butter
- For Filling
- 12-ounces cream cheese at room temp.
- Half a cup sugar
- Half a cup smooth peanut butter
- Quarter cup heavy cream
- 1 ½ tsp vanilla extract
- 1 tbsp all purpose flour
- 2 eggs at room temp.
- 1 egg yolk at room temp.
- ¾ cup choco-chips (semi-sweet)
- For Topping
- 180 ml milk chocolate, finely chopped
- 2/3 cup roughly chopped peanut butter cups
- 1/3 cup heavy cream

**Method:**

1. Arrange or make a 7" spring form pan by layering it with a non-stick spray.

2. Take a small bowl and mix butter and Oreo crumbs in it.

3. Spread it evenly in the up and bottom and in the sides of the pan.

4. Keep it in the freezer for 10 min.

5. Mix sugar and cream cheese in a mixing bowl at medium speed and add heavy cream, peanut butter, flour and vanilla in it.

6. Keep adding the eggs in it one by one for perfect blend. Do not over-mix this whole mixture.

7. Now add and stir the chocolate chips.

8. Pour the batter in the spring foam pan on the crust top. Then, cover the top of the pan with aluminium foil.

9. Pour two cups of water in the pressure cooker pot and keep the trivet at the bottom.

10. Cautiously keep the filled pan in the centre on the foil ling and sink it in the pressure cooker pot.

11. Fold down the foil sling so that it does not hamper the lid closing.

12. Grip the lid in place. Select the 'High Pressure' in your electric cooker and set 50 min.

13. Turn off the pressure cooker on the sound of beep.

14. For 10 minutes, use the natural pressure release and then do the quick pressure release to release any remaining pressure.

15. Carefully remove the lid when the valve drops.

16. Lift the cheesecake and see if the cheesecake is set in the middle.

17. In case it is not, cook the cheesecake for extra 5 minutes.

18. Remove the spring form pan for a wire rack to cool.

19. Take out the aluminium foil.

20. On cooling of the cheesecake, refrigerate it covered in plastic wrap for minimum 4 hours or over-night.

21. Prepare the topping when the cheesecake is chilled.

22. Keep half of the chocolate in a mixing bowl.

23. Put the heavy cream on medium heat till it starts boiling.

24. Then remove it from heat and instantly pour cream on the chocolate and mix till the chocolate is totally melted.

25. Cool it till the ganache gets thickened but is still thin enough to dribble down the cheesecake sides.

26. Embrace the chocolate ganache on the cheesecake top, extending to border outline and letting the ganache dribble down the sides.

27. Heap roughly chopped peanut butter cup chocolates on the top.

28. Refrigerate till it is ready to be served.

29. Make a hurl with a 20" piece of aluminium foil, folded 3 times length wise.

# Cooker samoa cheesecake

**Ingredients:**

**For Crust**

- Half a cup crushed chocolate graham cracker cookies
- 2 tbsp melted butter
- For Filling
- 12 ounces cream cheese at room temp.
- Half cup sugar
- Quarter cup heavy cream
- Quarter cup sour cream
- 1 ½ tsp vanilla extract
- 1 tbsp all purpose flour
- 1 egg yolk at room temp
- 2 eggs at room temp
- For Topping
- 1 ½ cups sweetened cut coconut
- 12 chewy unwrapped caramels, (Kraft preferred)
- 3 tbsp heavy cream
- Quarter cup semisweet chopped chocolate

**Method:**

1. Arrange or make a 7" spring form pan by layering it with a non-stick spray.

2. Mix butter and graham cracker crumbs in a small bowl.

3. Spread it evenly in the upside and bottom side and in the sides of the pan.

4. Keep it in the freezer for 10 min.

5. Mix sugar and cream cheese in a mixing bowl at medium speed and add heavy cream, sour cream, flour and vanilla in it.

6. Keep adding the eggs in it one by one for perfect blend. Do not over-mix this whole mixture.

7. Pour the batter in the spring form pan on the crust top.

8. Cover the spring form top with an aluminium foil.

9. Pour two cups of water in the pressure cooker pot and keep the trivet at the bottom.

10. Cautiously keep the filled pan in the centre on the foil ling and sink it in the pressure cooker pot.

11. Fold down the foil sling so that it does not hamper the lid closing.

12. Grip the lid in place. Select the 'High Pressure' in your electric cooker and set 35 min. Timer.

13. Turn off the pressure cooker on the sound of the beep.

14. For 10 minutes, use the natural pressure release and then do the quick pressure release to release any remaining pressure.

15. Carefully remove the lid when the valve drops.

16. Lift the cheesecake and see if the cheesecake is set in the middle.

17. In case it is not, cook the cheesecake for an extra 5 minutes.

18. Remove the spring form pan to cool the wire rack.

19. Remove the aluminium foil.

20. On cooling of the cheesecake, refrigerate it covered in plastic wrap for minimum 4 hours or over-night.

21. Prepare the topping when the cheesecake is chilled.

22. Preheat the oven to a temperature of 300 degrees. Evenly spread the coconut on a baking sheet and toast for 20 min.

23. Stir frequently until the coconut turns golden in colour and then cool on the baking sheet.

24. Place cream and caramels in a microwave-safe bowl when the coconut is cool.

25. Spread the topping carefully and evenly over the cheesecake top.

26. Melt the chocolate in the 50% power microwave safe bowl. Keep continuous stirring.

27. Keep it in a small Ziploc bag when it is melted and snip off a small piece of the corner of the bag.

28. Drop over the caramel topping top.

29. Make a heave with a 20 inch aluminium foil, folded 3 times in length.

# Mango Coconut Bread Pudding

**Ingredients:**

- 1 tbsp unsalted and melted butter

- 6 cups of bread cubes made from other bread with dense texture or challah bread

- 1 mango (about 500 grams), ripe but firm, peeled and cut into half inches cubes (quantity- 2 cups)

- 1/3 cup sweetened shredded/flaked coconut

- 5 large eggs

- 1 ½ cups low fat evaporated milk (one Twelve-ounce can) (not reconstituted)

- Half cup packed brown sugar

- 1 ½ cups coconut milk

- Half tsp ground cinnamon

- Half tsp ground ginger

- 2 tsp pure vanilla extract

- Half tsp ground allspice

**Method:**

1. Cover a 2 ¼ ceramic soufflé dish with melted butter (8 inch diameter) and keep.

2. Cut an aluminium foil piece (16" square) and butter an 8" round in the centre of it lightly.

3. Cut a 24" aluminium foil in length.

4. Fold it in half lengthwise and then again fold it in half 2 more times to make a strip about 24" long and 2 inches broad for making a "cradle" and keep.

5. Take a large bowl filled with mango, bread cubes and coconut.

6. Take a medium bowl filled with eggs.

7. Whisk it till it gets smooth.

8. Add coconut milk, evaporated milk, vanilla, brown sugar, ginger, cinnamon and allspice.

9. Whip to combine.

10. Pour bread cube mixture on it and gently stir.

11. Pour into made soufflé dish and let it stand half an hour at room temperature.

12. Cover it up with prepared foil sheet which is buttered on the down side for it to allow the bread pudding top to expand, but fits firmly around the soufflé dish sides.

13. In the middle of your folded foil strips, set the dish and bring the sides up twisting them together to form a handle.

14. Keep the rack in the cooking pot of the cooker.

15. Add 2 cups of cold water in it.

16. Use the foil cradle to aid lift the dish, cautiously lower the dish in the pot and keep it on the rack/trivet.

17. Cover the lid and lock it in place.

18. Choose 'High Pressure' and set the timer for 25 min.

19. Use the Natural Pressure Release for releasing pressure on hearing the beep sound.

20. Turn the float valve off when it drops.

21. Remove the lid, bending away from you for allowing the dispersion of steam.

22. Remove the bread pudding from the cooking pot with the help of foil strips for lifting up.

23. Keep it on a cooling rack.

24. Remove the foil

25. Let it stand for 10 minutes before serving or let it cool at room temp. Then cover and put for refrigeration.

26. It is ready to be served with softly whipped cream if liked.

# Ginger Steamed Pears and Vanilla Bean Mascarpone Cream

**Ingredients:**

- Vanilla bean mascarpone cream
- Quarter cup granulated sugar
- 1 cup medium dry sherry
- 2 strips lemon zest (about 2 strips of half inches each)
- 1 tbsp fresh lemon juice
- 4 to 5 slices of fresh ginger
- 4 pears, about 8-10 ounces each
- Half whole lemon
- Candied ginger or chocolate shavings and fresh raspberries for garnishing

**Method:**

1. Make Vanilla bean mascarpone cream.
2. Cover it up and refrigerate till the time it is ready to be used.
3. Take out of the refrigerator half an hour before serving.
4. Place sugar, sherry, lemon juice, lemon zest and ginger in the cooking pot of your electric pressure cooker.

5. Select 'Simmer' and cook it till the sugar is dissolved.

6. Pull out a slice from the bottom of every pear and use a small melon baller for removing the core.

7. Vertically peel the pear, leaving the stripes of the peel on the pear.

8. Stroke the cut surfaces with lemon half.

9. Place rack/trivet in cooking pot of your electric pressure cooker.

10. Use the lemon half to rub the cut surfaces.

11. Place rack/trivet in the cooking pot of your electric pressure cooker.

12. Keep the heatproof 8 inch plate on the trivet and arrange pears on it.

13. Select 'High Pressure' and keep it for cooking for 4 min.

14. Use the Natural Pressure Release for releasing pressure on hearing the beep sound.

15. Remove plate, pears and trivet.

16. Add any liquid which has acquired on the plate in the cooking liquid.

17. Let the pears cool and then cover and refrigerate until it is ready to be served.

18. Select the simmer and cook the liquid for 20-25 minutes approx. until it is decreased by 1/2. You should have a little more than half cup after decreasing.

19. Filter and cool.

20. Place the pears on different dessert plates.

21. Dribble with chilled ginger syrup and do the garnishing with fresh raspberries, a little lump of Vanilla Bean Mascarpone Cream and candied ginger and chocolate shavings.

22. You may stuff the hollow of the pear if you desire with Vanilla Bean Mascarpone Cream.

# Vanilla Bean Mascarpone Cream

## Ingredients:

- Half vanilla bean
- 8 ounces of softened at room temperature mascarpone cheese
- 1 tbsp powdered sugar
- 2 tsp milk
- Half tsp pure vanilla extract

## Method:

1. Break up the vanilla bean in ½ lengthwise.
2. Remove the outer layer of the seeds with the back side of the knife.
3. Place cheese, vanilla seeds, sugar, vanilla and milk in a small bowl.
4. Mix up with a whisk until it gets smooth. You can use either a food processor, hand mixer or a hand mixer for this purpose.
5. Put it for refrigeration until it is ready to be served.
6. Take out from the refrigerator half an hour before using it for it to get softened.
7. Vanilla Bean Mascarpone Cream can be used with ginger steamed pears.

# Conclusion

In simple words, cooking with an electric pressure cooker makes tasty food in less time and is very energy efficient. It helps in retaining the quality of the food you cook, cooking quicker using very little water.

With pressure cooking, natural flavors are at times intense so use lesser salt in your cooking and many grains and legumes get cooked faster and are easily digestible.

Enjoy!!!

# Do you want more books?

How would you like books arriving in your inbox each week?

They're FREE!

We publish books on all sorts of non-fiction niches and send them to our subscribers each week to spread the love.

All you have to do is sign up and you're good to go!

Just go to the link below, sign up, sit back and wait for your book downloads to arrive.

We couldn't have made it any easier. Enjoy!

www.LibraryBugs.com

Printed in Great Britain
by Amazon